BEAT THE WHEAT!

Easy and Delicious Wheat-free Recipes for Kids With Allergies

by KATRINA JORGENSEN

CONSULTANT
Amy Durkan MS, RDN, CDN
Nutrition Research Manager
Mount Sinai Medical Center
New York, NY, USA

raintree
a Capstone company — publishers for children

Raintree is an imprint of Capstone Global Library Limited, a company incorporated in
England and Wales having its registered office at 264 Banbury Road, Oxford, OX2 7DY –
Registered company number: 6695582

www.raintree.co.uk
myorders@raintree.co.uk

Edited by Anna Butzer
Designed by Heidi Thompson
Picture research by Morgan Walters
Production by Kathy McColley

ISBN 978 1 4747 1071 8 (hardback)
20 19 18 17 16
10 9 8 7 6 5 4 3 2 1

ISBN 978 1 4747 1076 3 (paperback)
21 20 19 18 17
10 9 8 7 6 5 4 3 2 1

British Library Cataloguing in Publication Data
A full catalogue record for this book is available from the British Library.

Design Elements
Shutterstock: avian, design element, Katerina Kirilova, design element, Lena Pan, design
element, Marco Govel, design element, mexrix, design element, Sabina Pittak, design
element, STILLFX, design element, swatchandsoda, design element

Photography by Capstone Studio: Karon Dubke

Editor's note:
Capstone cannot ensure that any food is allergen-free. The only way to be sure a food is
safe is to read all labels carefully, every time. Cross-contamination is also a risk for those
with food allergies. Please phone food companies to make sure their manufacturing
processes avoid cross-contamination. Also, always make sure you clean hands, surfaces
and tools before cooking.

CONTENTS

WHAT IS A FOOD ALLERGY?

Our bodies are armed with immune systems. It's the immune system's job to fight infections, viruses and invaders. Sometimes the immune system identifies a particular food as one of these invaders and attacks it. While our immune system fights, a chemical response is triggered and causes an allergic reaction. Reactions vary greatly from a mild skin irritation to having trouble breathing. Whenever you feel you are having a reaction, tell an adult immediately.

The best way to avoid having an allergic reaction is to be aware of what you are eating. Be careful not to consume that allergen. If you are not sure if that allergen is in a food, ask an adult or read the ingredients label of the food container before eating. Unfortunately, allergens can sometimes be hard to identify in an ingredient list. Have a look at www.coeliac.org.uk/gluten-free-diet-and-lifestyle/food-shopping/food-labels for a full list of hidden wheat terms.

Avoiding food allergens can be hard to do, especially when they are found in so many of our favourite foods. This cookbook will take you on a culinary journey to explore many of the dishes you've had to avoid because of a wheat allergy.

Kitchen safety

A safe kitchen is a fun kitchen! Always start your recipes with clean hands, surfaces and tools. Wash your hands and any tools you may use in future steps of a recipe, especially when handling raw meat. Make sure you have an adult nearby to help you with any task you don't feel comfortable doing, such as cutting vegetables or carrying hot pans.

ALLERGY ALERTS AND TIPS

Have other food allergies? No problem.
Have a look at the list at the end of each recipe
for substitutions for other common allergens.
Look out for other cool tips and ideas too!

CONVERSIONS

1/4 teaspoon	1.25 grams or millilitres
1/2 teaspoon	2.5 g or mL
1 teaspoon	5 g or mL
1 tablespoon	15 g or mL
10 grams	1/3 ounce
50 grams	1 3/4 oz
100 grams	3 1/2 oz
455 grams	16 oz (1 pound)
10 mL	1/3 fluid oz
50 mL	1 3/4 fl oz
100 mL	3 1/2 fl oz

Fahrenheit (°F)	Celsius (°C)
325°	160°
350°	180°
375°	190°
400°	200°
425°	220°
450°	230°

FLUFFY

Looking for a hearty breakfast that's quick, easy and wheat free? These pancakes stack up to their name – light, airy and delicious! Ditch the wheat with this breakfast delight, and don't forget the maple syrup!

Preparation time: 5 minutes

Cooking time: 10 minutes

Serves 4

Ingredients

250 grams wheat-free plain flour

2 teaspoons baking powder

2 tablespoons granulated sugar

pinch of salt

240 millilitres buttermilk

1 egg

2 tablespoons oil

1 teaspoon vanilla extract

cooking spray

maple syrup, for serving

Tools

measuring spoons/scales/jug

large mixing bowl

electric hand mixer with whisk
attachment

non-stick frying pan

spatula

plate

Allergen alert!

If you're avoiding dairy, you can make your
own dairy-free buttermilk! Simply mix
1 tablespoon lemon juice with 240 mL
dairy-free milk such as almond or rice milk.
Allow mixture to sit for five minutes and
then stir before adding to the recipe!

No eggs? No problem. Instead of
an egg, use one mashed-up banana.

1. Combine the flour, baking powder, sugar, salt, buttermilk, egg, oil and vanilla extract in a large bowl.

2. Mix the ingredients until mostly smooth using an electric hand mixer set on medium.

3. Place the non-stick frying pan on the hob on medium heat and spray lightly with cooking spray.

4. Spoon about 80 millilitres onto the hot pan.

5. Flip the pancake over when bubbles start to form around the edges of the pancake.

6. Continue cooking an additional two minutes or until golden brown on both sides.

7. Place cooked pancake on a plate and set aside.

8. Repeat steps 4 to 6 until all batter is used up.

9. Serve hot with maple syrup.

PUMPKIN MORNING MUFFINS

Pumpkins may be a staple of Halloween, but with this recipe, you can enjoy them all year round! This festive sweet treat is packed with Vitamin A, an essential nutrient that keeps your vision sharp.

Preparation time: 15 minutes

Cooking time: 30 minutes

Makes 12 muffins

Ingredients

1 tart apple, such as Granny Smith

2 carrots

80 millilitres oil

425 grams pumpkin puree

55 grams sugar

50 grams brown sugar

1 teaspoon maple extract

500 grams wheat-free plain flour

2 teaspoons bicarbonate of soda

1 teaspoon ground cinnamon

½ teaspoon ground ginger

¼ teaspoon ground cloves

¼ teaspoon salt

75 grams raisins

Tools

standard muffin tin with 12 cups

muffin cases

chopping board

vegetable peeler

chef's knife

spoon

box grater

large mixing bowl

measuring spoons/scales/jug

1. Preheat oven to 180°C. Place one case in each of the cups of the muffin tin and set aside.

2. Peel the apple with the vegetable peeler. Then cut out the core by cutting the apple in half from top to bottom. Chop the apple into small cubes and set aside.

3. Peel the carrots with the vegetable peeler. Grate the carrots using the large-holed side of a box grater. Set aside.

4. In a large mixing bowl, combine the oil, pumpkin, sugar, brown sugar and maple extract. Stir to combine.

5. Add the flour, bicarbonate of soda, cinnamon, ginger, cloves and salt. Stir until all the flour is absorbed. It's OK if the mixture is a little lumpy.

6. Add the apples, carrots and raisins to the bowl and mix.

7. Scoop the batter evenly into the muffin tin, filling each case about two-thirds full.

8. Bake for 30–35 minutes, or until a toothpick inserted into the centre of a muffin comes out clean.

CHEF'S TIP

Freeze leftover muffins and grab one in the morning for a quick on-the-go breakfast!

Allergens eradicated!

No major food allergens found here!

MAPLE SAUSAGE BITES

Good (and delicious) things come in small packages! Shop-bought sausages often use wheat as a filler, but these homemade bites are wheat free. Spicy and sweet flavours combine in these tiny breakfast sausages.

Preparation time: 15 minutes

Cooking time: 10 minutes

Serves 4

Ingredients

455 grams pork or turkey mince

½ teaspoon dried sage

½ teaspoon Italian seasoning

¼ teaspoon allspice

½ teaspoon seasoning salt

¼ teaspoon ground black pepper

1 teaspoon fennel seeds

1 teaspoon pure maple syrup

Tools

mixing bowl

measuring spoons/scales

fork

non-stick frying pan

spatula

Allergens eradicated!

No major food allergens found here!

1. Combine the pork or turkey mince, dried sage, Italian seasoning, allspice, seasoning salt, black pepper, fennel seeds and maple syrup in a mixing bowl.

2. Mix with a fork until well-blended.

3. Split the mixture into 12 equal pieces and form into small, flat, round patties.

4. Place a non-stick frying pan on the hob on medium heat.

5. Add 3 or 4 patties to the pan and cook until browned on one side, two to three minutes.

6. Using the spatula, flip the patties. Cook an additional two to three minutes, or until no longer pink inside.

7. Repeat steps 5 and 6 until all the patties are cooked.

8. Serve hot as a side to your favourite breakfast!

CHEF'S TIP

If you are worried your hands will get too sticky handling the sausage mixture, rub a little oil on your palms beforehand!

RAISIN **GRANOLA**

It's important to eat breakfast before you start your day, but that can be tough when so many breakfast foods – especially cereal – contain wheat. With this recipe, you not only get a healthy substitute for cereal, you can take the leftovers with you for an on-the-go snack!

Preparation time: 10 minutes

Cooking time: 20 minutes

Serves 4

Ingredients

200 grams wheat-free rolled oats

15 grams wheat-free rice cereal

1 teaspoon ground cinnamon

¼ teaspoon salt

2 tablespoons brown sugar

105 grams pure maple syrup

80 millilitres oil, such as light olive oil

½ teaspoon vanilla

150 grams raisins

Tools

large baking tray

baking parchment

mixing bowl

measuring spoons/scales/jug

spatula

1. Preheat oven to 165°C. Place a sheet of baking parchment on a large baking tray and set aside.

2. Combine the rolled oats, rice cereal, ground cinnamon, salt, brown sugar, maple syrup, oil, vanilla and raisins in a mixing bowl. Stir until the ingredients are coated well.

3. Spread the granola mixture on the baking tray so it is mostly flat.

4. Bake in the oven for 20 minutes or until slightly golden brown.

5. Remove from the oven and allow to cool before serving.

6. Eat with your favourite yogurt, or splash some milk on top for a crunchy breakfast treat!

7. Store leftovers in an airtight container for up to two weeks.

Allergens eradicated!

No major food allergens found here!

CHEF'S TIP

Do raisins wrinkle your nose? Add any of your favourite dried fruits to this granola instead, such as blueberries, cherries, apricots or bananas!

CREAMY
MAC and CHEESE

Does your mouth water at the thought of ooey, gooey cheese? If so, then this recipe is for you! Satisfy your comfort food craving with a bowl of this delicious pasta dish that is rich in calcium.

Preparation time: 15 minutes

Cooking time: 15 minutes

Serves 4

Ingredients

225 grams mature cheddar cheese

1.9 litres water

2 teaspoons salt

200 grams dry wheat-free pasta, such as rice pasta

30 grams butter

2 tablespoons rice flour

480 millilitres milk

¼ teaspoon ground mustard

¼ teaspoon paprika

Tools

box grater

chopping board

large saucepan

measuring spoons/scales/jug

medium saucepan

whisk

colander

spoon

1. Grate the cheese with a large-holed grater set on top of a chopping board. Set aside.

2. In the large saucepan, add the water and salt. Place on the hob on high heat until the water begins to boil.

3. Add the wheat-free pasta. Reduce the heat to medium-high. Cook according to package directions until just tender.

4. Make cheese sauce while the pasta cooks. In the saucepan, melt butter over medium heat.

5. Add the rice flour and whisk until absorbed. The mixture should look like wet sand.

6. Slowly pour the milk in while whisking to avoid lumps. Bring the mixture to a gentle simmer. Keep whisking until it begins to thicken, about five minutes.

7. Stir in the cheese, ground mustard and paprika until melted. If the sauce is too thick, add a bit of milk.

8. When the pasta is done, drain it in a colander and place back into the large saucepan.

9. Pour the cheese sauce over the pasta and stir until coated with the sauce.

10. Serve hot in bowls.

Allergen alert!

Cheese, butter and milk a no-go? You can still achieve cheesy greatness by using your favourite dairy-free cheese, butter and milk replacements.

CHEF'S TIP

Add your favourite vegetables or toppings such as broccoli, carrots, asparagus, tomatoes, bacon, chicken or beef!

TACO LETTUCE CUPS

Some taco shells contain wheat, but that doesn't mean you have to take tacos off the menu! Using round lettuce leaves as the shells, you can whip up some tasty tacos in no time! Top these leafy "shells" with your favourite veggies and taco toppings!

Preparation time: 20 minutes

Cooking time: 15 minutes

Serves 4

Ingredients

455 grams lean beef or turkey mince

1 tablespoon chilli powder

1 teaspoon ground cumin

½ teaspoon ground oregano

½ teaspoon paprika

½ teaspoon black pepper

¼ teaspoon onion powder

¼ teaspoon garlic powder

1 teaspoon salt

1 head round lettuce

Taco fillings

sweetcorn

beans

tomatoes

avocados

onion

your favourite cheese

salsa

Tools

frying pan

spoon

measuring spoons/scales

kitchen roll

chopping board

chef's knife

serving bowls

1. In a frying pan, brown the beef or turkey mince over medium heat, breaking up the meat into small pieces with a spoon.

2. Add the chilli powder, cumin, oregano, paprika, black pepper, onion powder, garlic powder and salt. Stir to combine and reduce heat to low.

3. Carefully remove the outer leaves from the head of lettuce and dispose of them. Pull off 12 leaves and wash them gently under cool running water. Pat them dry with the kitchen roll and set aside.

4. Prepare your taco fillings by chopping tomatoes into small pieces, dicing the avocado, cutting the onion and grating the cheese. Place in bowls for serving.

5. Transfer the meat to a serving bowl and scoop about 2 tablespoons of meat into each lettuce cup. Then add fillings to your liking.

6. Wrap up tightly and enjoy.

CHEF'S TIP

Vegetarians, don't fret! You can skip the meat and use one tin of drained black beans instead. You can also use 500 grams of chopped aubergine or butternut squash in step 1.

Allergens eradicated!

No major food allergens found here!

CHICKEN COURGETTI SOUP

When you're feeling under the weather, nothing beats a piping hot bowl of chicken noodle soup. However, most types of pasta are made with wheat. To avoid wheat, make the change from noodles to courgette spaghetti!

Preparation time: 20 minutes

Cooking time: 1½ hours

Serves 4

Ingredients

455 grams chicken leg quarters

1.9 litres water

2 carrots

2 stalks celery

1 small onion

1 tablespoon dried parsley

2 teaspoons salt

1 teaspoon black pepper

1 teaspoon garlic powder

1 teaspoon ground turmeric

½ teaspoon dried thyme

½ teaspoon dried oregano

1 large courgette

Tools

large stockpot

measuring spoons/scales/jug

vegetable peeler

chopping board

chef's knife

tongs

box grater

2 forks

Allergens eradicated!

No major food allergens found here!

1. Place the chicken and water in a large stockpot. Set the pot on the hob on medium-high heat until it begins to simmer. Reduce heat to medium and cook for about one hour until the meat is cooked.

2. Prepare the vegetables while the meat cooks. Peel the carrots with a vegetable peeler. Chop the carrots and celery into 0.6-centimetre (¼-inch) rounds. Cut the onion in half, peel and then chop into small pieces. Set aside.

3. After the meat is cooked, carefully remove it from the pot using tongs. Place on a chopping board to cool.

4. Add the carrots, celery, onion, dried parsley, salt, pepper, garlic powder, turmeric, thyme and oregano to the liquid and stir. Increase heat to bring to a low boil. Then reduce heat to medium and cook for about 30 minutes.

5. While the vegetables cook, grate the courgette with the large-holed side of a box grater. Set aside.

6. Carefully pull the meat off the bones (use two forks to avoid burning your fingers). Set aside.

7. Add both the courgette and chicken back to the liquid. Stir for about one minute until the courgette is cooked.

8. Serve hot in bowls with wheat-free bread, if desired.

CHEF'S TIP

Craving carbs? Add 200 grams rice to the pot during step 4.

CHICKEN PARMESAN
STUFFED PEPPERS

What do you get when you cross chicken Parmesan and stuffed peppers? Two mouthwatering entrees rolled into one! Wheat-free breadcrumbs top off this recipe to give it a delightful crunch.

Preparation time: 20 minutes

Cooking time: 30 minutes

Serves 4

Ingredients

455 grams chicken breasts

½ teaspoon salt

¼ teaspoon pepper

3 teaspoons olive oil

4 bell peppers

255 grams marinara sauce

4 slices mozzarella cheese

50 grams Parmesan cheese

25 grams wheat-free breadcrumbs

Tools

chopping board

chef's knife

measuring spoons/scales

frying pan

small mixing bowl

spoon

20 x 20-cm (8 x 8-in) baking dish

Allergen alert!

You can still go Italian without all the cheese. Skip the mozzarella and replace the Parmesan with 57 grams nutritional yeast for a cheesy flavour without the dairy!

1. Preheat oven to 180°C.

2. Cut the chicken breasts in 2.5-centimetre (1-inch) cubes. Sprinkle salt and pepper on the cubes and set aside.

3. Place 2 teaspoons olive oil in a frying pan and place on the hob on medium heat.

4. Add the chicken and cook until no longer pink inside, about five to six minutes.

5. While the chicken cooks, cut off the tops of the bell peppers and scoop out the seeds and white ribs inside.

6. Pour the marinara sauce in with the chicken and stir until coated.

7. Place 1 slice of mozzarella cheese in the bottom of each pepper.

8. Evenly scoop the chicken into each pepper.

9. In a small bowl, combine the Parmesan cheese, breadcrumbs and 1 teaspoon olive oil and stir.

10. Sprinkle the breadcrumb mixture evenly over the top of each pepper.

11. Place the peppers in the baking dish. Bake for about 30 minutes or until the peppers are slightly tender and topping is golden brown.

12. Serve hot.

SWEET POTATO

SHEPHERD'S PIE

Warm and comforting, this dish is
sure to satisfy your hunger. As an
added bonus, it is also rich in vitamins
and protein. Have fun serving up a
sweetened, wheat-free spin on this
English classic.

Preparation time: 15 minutes

Cooking time: 1 hour

Serves 4

Ingredients

4 medium sweet potatoes

1.9 litres water

1 small onion

1 teaspoon olive oil

455 grams lean beef or turkey mince

240 millilitres beef broth

1 teaspoon coconut aminos

1 tablespoon tomato paste

1 teaspoon garlic powder

60 grams butter

1 teaspoon salt

½ teaspoon ground black pepper

¼ teaspoon paprika

455 grams frozen vegetable mix
  (carrots, corn, peas)

Tools

vegetable peeler

chef's knife

chopping board

measuring spoons/scales/jug

medium saucepan

large frying pan

spoon

colander

potato masher

20 x 20-cm (8 x 8-in) baking dish

spatula

1. Preheat oven to 165°C.

2. Peel and chop the potatoes. Place them in the saucepan and fill with water. Place on the hob on high heat and boil. Reduce heat to medium and cook for 15 minutes or until tender.

3. Peel and chop the onion. Set aside.

4. Place frying pan on the hob and set to medium heat. Add oil and onions. Cook for two minutes, stirring gently.

5. Place meat in frying pan and break up into small pieces with a spoon. Cook until no longer pink, about eight minutes.

6. Add the broth, aminos, tomato paste and garlic powder to the frying pan. Stir to combine. Reduce heat to low and allow to simmer gently.

7. Drain the potatoes, return to pan and mash. Add butter, salt, pepper, and paprika. Mash until smooth.

8. Add frozen vegetables to the frying pan. Stir to combine.

9. Pour the meat mixture into the baking dish. Spread potatoes on top with a spatula.

10. Bake for 40 minutes, or until the top of the sweet potatoes is slightly browned.

11. Allow to cool for five minutes before serving hot in bowls.

CHEF'S TIP

Not sweet on sweet potatoes? You can use
normal white potatoes in this recipe instead.

BAKED FRENCH FRIES

High in Vitamin C and potassium, potatoes are a great addition to your daily intake. Baking these delicious French fries is more heart-healthy too! Grab some spuds and create your own homemade fries with this quick and simple recipe.

Preparation time: 15 minutes

Cooking time: 30 minutes

Serves 4

Ingredients

4 medium potatoes

2 tablespoons oil, such as olive oil

½ teaspoon salt

¼ teaspoon pepper

Tools

large baking tray

baking parchment

vegetable peeler

chopping board

chef's knife

kitchen roll

measuring spoons

mixing bowl

spatula

Allergens eradicated!

No major food allergens found here!

1. Preheat oven to 220°C. Line the baking tray with baking parchment. Set aside.

2. Peel the potatoes. Carefully cut each potato into three pieces lengthwise. Then cut each section into 4 or 5 pieces lengthwise, making long sticks.

3. Rinse the potato sticks and dry well with kitchen roll.

4. Place the sticks in the mixing bowl with the oil, salt and pepper. Toss gently to coat evenly.

5. Spread the sticks on the baking tray, making sure they are not stacked on top of each other.

6. Bake for about 15 minutes. Using a spatula, carefully flip over the fries. Bake an additional 15 minutes or until deep golden brown and crispy.

7. Remove from oven and allow to cool for five minutes before serving.

CHEF'S TIP

Get fancy with your fries
and add some fun flavours:
Italian fries: Add 1 teaspoon
Italian seasoning during step 4.
Spicy buffalo fries: Add ¼ teaspoon
cayenne pepper during step 4.

25

BLTA PASTA SALAD

You don't need to make a sandwich to enjoy the classic flavours of a BLT. Bacon, lettuce, tomato, avocado and pasta are the perfect players for a refreshing, scrumptious salad.

Preparation time: 3 hours 20 minutes (3 hours inactive)

Cooking time: 45 minutes

Serves 4

Ingredients

1.9 litres water

2 teaspoons salt

100 grams wheat-free pasta

2 tablespoons Dijon mustard

2 tablespoons apple cider vinegar

60 millilitres extra virgin olive oil

2 teaspoons honey

3 slices wheat-free bacon

2 tomatoes

1 head romaine lettuce

1 avocado

Tools

medium saucepan

measuring spoons/scales/jug

colander

medium bowl

small mixing bowl

whisk

frying pan

chopping board

chef's knife

large mixing bowl

tongs

Allergens eradicated!

No major food allergens found here!

1. Add water and salt to a saucepan and place on the hob on high heat to boil.
Add the pasta and cook according to package directions.

2. Drain the pasta and rinse with cool water.

3. Place pasta in a medium bowl. Cover and place in a refrigerator for at least three hours to cool completely.

4. While the pasta cools, make the dressing. In a small mixing bowl, combine the Dijon mustard, vinegar, olive oil and honey. Whisk quickly until it is smooth and no longer separated. Add salt if needed.

5. Cook the bacon in a frying pan until crisp. Chop the bacon on a chopping board. Set aside.

6. Chop the tomato and lettuce. Set aside.

7. With an adult's help, cut the avocado open and remove the pit. Scoop out the pulp and chop it. Set aside.

8. To assemble, put the cooled pasta, dressing, bacon, tomato, lettuce and avocado in a large mixing bowl. Toss gently with tongs.

9. Allow to rest about 15 minutes before serving. Store leftovers in a refrigerator for up to five days.

APPLE  CAKE

Apple pie is a British favourite, but have you ever tried apple cake? Besides being delicious, apples are also high in Vitamin C and fibre. Enjoy making this cake studded with pieces of autumn's favourite fruit!

Preparation time: 20 minutes

Cooking time: 45 minutes

Serves 6

Ingredients

cooking spray

245 grams wheat-free plain flour

1 teaspoon cinnamon

1 teaspoon bicarbonate of soda

1 teaspoon baking powder

¼ teaspoon salt

340 grams granulated sugar

175 millilitres light olive oil

1 teaspoon vanilla extract

3 eggs

3 tart apples

Tools

20 x 20-cm (8 x 8-in)
   cake tin

2 medium mixing bowls

measuring spoons/scales/jug

electric mixer

vegetable peeler

chopping board

chef's knife

toothpick

Allergen alert!

If you need to avoid eggs, substitute
370 grams apple sauce in the batter.

1. Preheat oven to 180°C. Spritz the cake tin lightly with cooking spray and set aside.

2. In a mixing bowl, combine the wheat-free flour, cinnamon, bicarbonate of soda, baking powder and salt.

3. In another mixing bowl, add the sugar, oil, vanilla extract and eggs.

4. Using an electric mixer set to medium speed, mix the wet ingredients until blended.

5. Pour the wet ingredients into the bowl with dry ingredients. Mix on medium speed until smooth. Set aside.

6. Peel the apples with a vegetable peeler. Chop into small pieces.

7. Transfer half of the batter into the cake tin. Evenly sprinkle apples on top. Pour the remaining batter over them.

8. Place in the oven and bake for about 45 minutes, or until a toothpick comes out clean when inserted.

CINNAMON  COOKIES

Sugar and spice and everything nice – and no wheat! Crispy on the outside, chewy on the inside, these cookies made with almond flour are easy to make and fun to eat!

Preparation time: 10 minutes

Cooking time: 25 minutes

Makes 12 cookies

Ingredients

190 grams almond flour

¼ teaspoon bicarbonate of soda

1½ teaspoons ground cinnamon

80 grams pure maple syrup

60 grams butter, softened to room temperature

Topping

½ teaspoon cinnamon

2 teaspoons granulated sugar

optional: almond slivers

Tools

large baking tray

baking parchment

mixing bowl

measuring spoons/scales

spoon

small mixing bowl

spatula

cooling rack

Allergen alert!

If you need to avoid dairy, substitute coconut oil for butter. The coconut oil will give the cookies a similar, yet tropical flavour!

If you have a nut allergy, use a wheat-free flour blend and leave the almond slivers off.

1. Preheat oven to 140°C. Line a large baking tray with baking parchment and set aside.

2. In a mixing bowl, combine the almond flour, bicarbonate of soda, ground cinnamon and maple syrup.

3. Add the butter and mix well. Use your hands if it gets difficult to stir.

4. Split the dough into 12 equal pieces. Roll each piece into a ball.

5. In a small mixing bowl, combine the cinnamon and sugar. Roll the dough balls around in the mixture to lightly coat.

6. Place the dough balls on the baking tray. Flatten them with the palm of your hand to make a circle shape. Place almond slivers on top if desired.

7. Place in the oven for about 15 minutes. Using a spatula, flip the cookies. Bake an additional 10 minutes.

8. Remove from oven. Allow to cool for five minutes before placing on a cooling rack.

9. Serve warm or at room temperature. Store leftovers in an airtight container for up to one week.

GLOSSARY

assemble put all the parts of something together

blend mix together, sometimes using a blender

boil heat until large bubbles form on top of a liquid; the boiling point for water is 100°C (212°F)

consume eat or drink something

mash smash a soft food into a lumpy mixture

pit single central seed or stone of some fruits

pulp soft juicy or fleshy part of a fruit or vegetable

simmer keep just below boiling when cooking or heating

whisk stir a mixture rapidly until it's smooth

READ MORE

Allergy-free Cooking for Kids, Pamela Clark (Sterling Epicure, 2014)

The Allergy-Free Family Cookbook, Fiona Heggie and Ellie Lux (Orion, 2015)

The Kids Only Cookbook, Sue Quinn (Quadrille Publishing, 2013)

WEBSITE

www.allergyuk.org
If you have any allergies, this is the website to go to. It provides lots of useful information and a helpline.